Understanding Machiavelli's *The Prince*

© Max Milo éditions, Paris, 2023
"Comprendre/Essai graphique"
www.maxmilo.com
ISBN 978-2-315-01259-6

Denis Collin - Laura Acquaviva

Understanding Machiavelli's *The Prince*

Comprendre/essai graphique

Introduction:
Machiavelli's Bad Reputation

Politics gets a bad press. Broken promises, blatant lies, dirty tricks - isn't that what politics is all about, which is why it's often said that "everyone's rotten"? And when politics becomes philosophy, the villain is Machiavelli. Wasn't the Florentine secretary the theorist of lying in politics? Isn't the cunning politician, the one who lies to all and sundry in order to achieve his ends and gain and keep power, "Machiavellian"? Indeed, with Machiavelli, it seems that politics and morality don't mix. And against *"messer Niccolò"*, the great air of slander can be played *ad libitum*. In Machiavelli's defense, however, we can call a few prestigious witnesses.

Let's start with Spinoza, a friend of truth if ever there was one. A common thread runs through his

Treatise on Politics: the reference to the man he calls "the most penetrating Florentine", whose lessons based on experience are better followed than the lamentations of theologians, moralists and other misanthropes, all those individuals who refuse to treat men as they are.

Now let's call on Jean-Jacques Rousseau, the good Jean-Jacques Rousseau, enemy of all the tricks that corrupt society is wont to pull. In The *Social Contract*, Rousseau does not spare the philosophers. Grotius and Hobbes take their toll. The only one to get off scot-free is the author of The *Prince*. In a note, he writes: "[...] it is natural that princes should always give preference to the maxim that is most immediately useful to them. This is what Samuel strongly represented to the Hebrews; this is what Machiavelli has made clear. By pretending to give lessons to kings, he gave great lessons to peoples. Machiavelli's *Prince* is the book of republicans" (*Du contrat social*, livre II, in *Œuvres* III, Gallimard, "La Pléiade", p. 409). We can also quote Hegel, who complains that "Machiavelli's voice has remained unheard". *The Prince* is not a satire, and Machiavelli must be taken seriously.

Introduction: Machiavelli's Bad Reputation

We could "kick the can down the road" by pointing out that *The Prince* alone does not sum up Machiavelli's thinking, which would turn him into a kind of two-faced Janus, on the one hand the cynic of The *Prince* and on the other the impeccable republican of the *Discourses on the First Decade of Titus Livius*. But there's no need to shy away. First, we need to understand the cursed *De principatibus*. And consider what it's really about: experimental science. And to be useful, the experiment must come as close as possible to the "actual truth of the thing". Far from writing a manual of political cunning and cynicism, Machiavelli's aim is both moral and scientific: to tell the truth about politics. A great expert in disillusionment, he invites us to face up not only to political reality, but also to human reality, not to abandon all hope, as at the entrance to Dante's Inferno, but to think seriously about action, as in chapter XXVI, where Machiavelli calls for "liberating Italy from the Barbarians". For to fight barbarism, we need neither words nor fine sentiments, but the truth, however bitter it may be.

Understanding Machiavelli's The Prince

The Prince, A Foundational Book of Modern Political Thought

Niccolò Machiavelli was born in Florence in 1469. He was the son of Bernardo Machiavelli, a landowner who usually lived in Sant'Andreà in Percussina, in the municipality of San Casciano, near Florence. The Machiavelli family is an old Florence family belonging to the bourgeoisie organized in the seven "major arts". Since the middle of the 13th century, it has lost a good part of its fortune, but it continues to provide Florence with those honest civil servants, scribes and accountants who maintain the continuity of the republic through the ups and downs of often turbulent public life, pulled in all directions by the struggle of parties and wealthy families such as the all-powerful Medici family.

Understanding Machiavelli's The Prince

The Prince, A Foundational Book of Modern Political Thought

Machiavelli's life is closely linked to the last decades of the Republic of Florence. Just a few years after his death in 1527, the Tuscan republics (Florence and Siena) came under the control of the Medici family, who ruled the "Grand Duchy of Tuscany". In 1494, French armies raided Italy for the first time. The whole of Tuscany was caught up in the turmoil. When Charles VIII's armies reached Florence, a popular uprising drove out the Medici, who had ruled the city since 1434 under the guise of republican institutions. A preacher-monk, Girolamo Savonarola, became the spokesman for the popular movement and de facto leader of the republic. Under his leadership, a reform of the institutions was undertaken with the creation of the "Grand Council", which allowed for greater popular participation in government. Supported initially by the people, Savonarola advocated a moral reform that led him to break with the papacy. He was excommunicated in 1497 by Alexander VI Borgia. In early 1498, however, public opinion began to turn, and Savonarola was soon pursued, arrested, tried and sentenced to the stake.

Machiavelli remained aloof from the turmoil. In 1498, when the "republican party" regained the upper hand, the new "gonfalonier of justice", Piero Soderini, appointed Machiavelli secretary of the second chancellery of the republic of Florence on May 25, 1498 (five days after Savonarola's execution). On July 14 of the same year, he was placed at the disposal of the Ten of Balia, a council appointed to administer the republic in exceptional situations. Machiavelli soon became an unofficial diplomat. He undertook numerous missions on behalf of the Florentine Republic, notably to France, Germany and the other city-states of northern Italy. One such mission sent him to Caesar Borgia, Duke of Valentinois, who was trying to restore order to one of the Papacy's dependent states, Romagna. It was a decisive meeting that gave Machiavelli the opportunity to observe a "prince", but it was also the source of many misunderstandings, as Machiavelli came to be seen as a sort of theorist of Caesar Borgia's abuses.

He was involved in Florence's domestic politics, writing some of the gonfalonier's speeches, in particular with a view to raising a special tax to finance Florence's defense. He also witnessed the new "descent" of the French into Italy, with the ensuing unrest between Italian cities. He drew an important conclusion: Italy's misfortune stemmed from discord, and the invaders were "barbarians" who needed to be liberated.

In 1512, Spanish, Venetian, Swiss and Papal troops invaded the Arno plain: the inhabitants of Prato were massacred (August 29). Although the seigneury under Soderini's leadership was clearly Francophile and had refused to join Julius II's League, an uprising, skilfully fomented by the Medici, overthrew the republican party. Piero Soderini fled. Medicean troops enter Florence. The Great Council and the Council of Eighty are abolished. Legislative and executive powers were entrusted to a committee of sixty-five representatives of Florence's main aristocratic families. The leaders and collaborators of the overthrown power were impeached. Machiavelli tasted prison. In 1513, a general amnesty released him, but he was barred from all public functions and had to settle for the life of a country gentleman, sharing Chianti wine with the peasants and artisans who frequented the inn near his home, the *Albergaccio* de Sant'Andreà in Percussina. It was here that he set about writing an "opuscule *De principatibus*", as he wrote to Francesco Vettori on December 10, 1513: "I am digging into the problems posed by such a subject as best I can: debating what principality is[1], how many species there are, how it is acquired and how it is kept and why it is lost" (*The Prince*, in *Œuvres*, Éditions Robert Laffont, 2006, translation by Christian Bec, p. 1239).[2]

The work, which would become famous under the title of its posthumous edition, *Le Prince*, was dedicated first to Julien de Medici and then to the young Lorenzo Medici in an unsuccessful attempt to return to active politics. This firebrand, so often

---

[1]. Christian Bec translates the Latin "*De principatibus*" (*principato* in Italian) as "monarchies". We have taken the liberty of replacing "monarchy" with "principality".

[2]. All quotations from Machiavelli are taken from this edition. For these extracts, only the relevant page is indicated in brackets.

quoted, so often vilified and, in the end, so little read, was intended "to be agreeable to a prince, especially a new prince". It should enable its author to return to active politics: "As for this work, if one would only read it, one would see that during the fifteen years I devoted to State affairs, I neither slept nor spent my time playing. It should be taken to heart to use someone who has gained experience at the expense of others. My loyalty should not be questioned because, having always been loyal, I cannot now learn to be less so" (p. 1240).

At the same time, he was writing *Discours sur la première décade de Tite-Live*, a work that defended republican principles. But all we know of Machiavelli is *The Prince*, and, to be honest, all we know of it is its title and bad reputation: a manual of "Machiavellianism", i.e. cynicism or the uncontrolled use of "raison d'État". The Florentine secretary's "perfidious" or "perverse" theses - in short, his radical immoralism - are denounced as opposed to a law that transcends the political order.

Yet Machiavelli claims to be putting into this work the thing that is "dearest" to him, "knowledge of the actions of great men; knowledge that I have learned by long experience of modern things and continual reading of ancient ones" (p. 109). The circumstances of the work and its (unsuccessful) objective should not detract from its theoretical importance. It circulated in Florence in manuscript form as early as 1517. Printed in Rome in 1531, it was initially well received, before provoking violent reactions and numerous "refutations". Nevertheless, this work is one of the foundations of modern political thought.

The letter to Vettori dated December 10 clearly indicates the aim and content of the work. Firstly, to define what "principality" is (*"che cosa è principato"*); secondly, to find out how many kinds of such "principalities" exist; thirdly, to find out how they can be acquired; and, finally, for what reasons they are lost.

The Prince's rigorous composition follows this plan. The very brief introductory chapter I is followed by chapters II to XI, which deal with the various types of principalities (old, II to VI; new or acquired, VII to X; ecclesiastical, XI); chapters XII to XIV deal with the

The Prince, A Foundational Book of Modern Political Thought

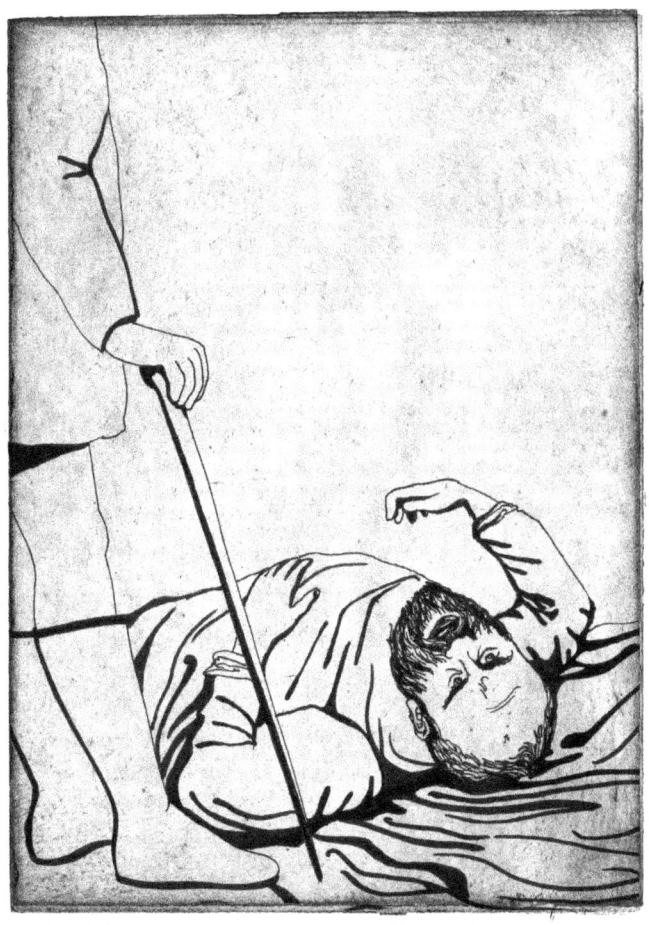

means of defense that princes must master; chapters XV to XXV deal with the behavior of the prince, and the concluding chapter XVI is an exhortation to seize Italy and drive out the barbarians, the higher task for which a new prince is needed.

The Prince begins with a dichotomous classification. Starting with the most general, the concept of *principality* is built up through successive refinements. The Latin title *De principatibus* can be translated as "of principalities" (or "of principates"). The two titles correspond: this is a treatise on principalities, which includes a treatise on princes, i.e. the qualities required of those who wish to govern a principality. At the most general level, we must distinguish all political regimes into two great classes, principalities and republics: "All powers which have had or which have authority over men are either republics or principalities" (p. 110).

There are also "civil principalities" that resemble republics. Moreover, traditionally, the term "republic" has been used to designate any government based on laws and the pursuit of the common good, and so a government in which one man holds primacy (a principality in the strict sense of the term) could well be republican. In the theory of mixed government, as formulated since Aristotle and Cicero, and taken up, in his own way, by Machiavelli, the republic thus constituted includes a monarchical or princely element. Machiavelli then distinguishes between two kinds of "principalities": "Principalities are either hereditary, where the lineage of their lord has long been sovereign, or they are new" (p. 110).

The important thing, however, is that new principalities are in turn divided into two categories: those that are entirely new, and those that are added to an existing principality. The dichotomy becomes more complex: new principalities, whether entirely new or not, are in turn divided into three times two sub-categories:

- those whose subjects have been accustomed to living free and those whose subjects are accustomed to living under the command of a prince;
- those acquired by one's own arms or by the arms of another ;
- those acquired by fortune or virtue.

In theory, then, the new principalities can be divided into eight categories, produced by combining the three dichotomous criteria we have just outlined. Chapter II is very brief, because the stability of hereditary principalities does not pose any serious problems.

The Hardest Part: Founding a New Principality

The difficulty lies in the new principalities. And it's in chapter III that we get to the heart of the matter. From hereditary principalities, we move on to mixed principalities, those which are hereditary but to which new possessions have been added. Their difficulties are, in fact, those of all new principalities, and, as always with Machiavelli, they have their origins in the nature of men: "[...] men willingly change master believing they will find better. This belief makes them take up arms against that master; in which they are mistaken, for they then see by experience that their condition has worsened" (p. 112). Remarks like these show just how much the Machiavelli of the *Prince* is the man who defends republican freedom in the *Discourses*:

as soon as men have a master, they have a bad master, and if they change it's for an even worse one... Implicit conclusion: if you're dissatisfied with your master, become free citizens! And this is the underlying discourse throughout The *Prince*.

In any case, this rule, empirically verifiable if Machiavelli is to be believed, has an explanation. It stems from a "natural and ordinary necessity": "one must always bully those whose new prince one becomes". This "natural necessity" can be explained as follows: the conqueror must bully those who didn't want him - that's obvious. But neither can he please those who brought him in, who are always bound to be disappointed, nor can he bully them completely, since he is their obligator. In other words, the prince is condemned to displease all factions, but in the case of mixed principalities, he must also have allies, since it's a question of entering a country in which he has not hitherto been the prince, and this can only be done with "the favor of its inhabitants". Military art is never enough, and war is only one of the means of politics - politics pursued by other means, as Clausewitz would say.

The Hardest Part: Founding a New Principality

A second question faces the prince who annexes "new states". It is easier to annex states of "the same country and language" and "it is very easy to keep them, especially if they are not accustomed to living free" (p. 112). Machiavelli's indirect argument, then, is that the unification of "states" of "the same country and language" by its very ease is a more legitimate annexation - more legitimate, for example, than Louis XII's annexation of Milan. The various states that make up the *regnum italicum* (kingdom of Italy) are of the same country and language, and so a determined prince should succeed in unifying them. In short, beyond Italian communes and micro-states, Machiavelli turns his attention to the princes who achieved the unity of the great nations of Europe, the typical example being France (p. 113).

In other cases, difficulties necessarily multiply, and retaining these acquisitions requires a great deal of luck and a methodical policy of occupation, possibly including colonization. In fact, Machiavelli suggests that it is almost impossible to annex different peoples without crushing them: "Men must be either surrounded by friendliness or destroyed:

for they take revenge for light offenses; for serious ones they cannot; so that the offense done to them must be such that it does not deserve to be avenged" (p. 114).

However, the focus is on the Italian situation after the French invasion. Political thought is that of conjunctures, "the concrete analysis of concrete situations" as Lenin would say. For example, this comment on Louis XII's attempts to seize the kingdom of Naples: "The desire to conquer is a very natural and ordinary thing. When men who can do so experience it, they are always to be praised and not blamed; but when they can't and want to do it anyway, therein lies error and blame" (p. 116-117). Machiavelli is simply noting the common way in which historical events are judged. Conquerors who succeed and keep their conquests are praised. The conquest of England by a Norman prince belonging to a lineage that had forcibly settled in the kingdom of France is long since forgotten! On the other hand, the history books in use in the countries of Europe consider it a good thing that the Greeks repelled the Persians, that Charles Martel stemmed the Arab thrust or that some rather crude Spanish knights brought down the Arab-Muslim civilization of Andalusia. Machiavelli, as a moralist in the French 17th-century sense, analyzes political mores. Neither laughing nor crying, just understanding.

Republics have a Taste for Freedom

The history of ancient princes provides food for more general thought. Discussing the empire of Darius after the death of Alexander, Machiavelli distinguishes between two kinds of principalities: those based on a feudal order and feudal lords "who have a state and subjects of their own", and those "ruled by a prince and his servants" (p. 118). The latter have greater authority than the former, which is why their states are harder to conquer than feudal ones, but, once conquered, they are easier to keep. Subjects accustomed to the condition of slaves are quick to obey, even when they have changed masters. Conversely, the relative freedom of feudalism, with its quarrels between barons, makes lasting occupation of the country more difficult. But of course, it is in republics that the taste for freedom is strongest, and it is for this reason that they are the most difficult to keep permanently, for they "have more life, more hatred, more desire for revenge; the memory of their former freedom does not and cannot leave them in peace; so that the surest course is to destroy them or to remain in them" (p. 121).

This passage is a warning to the Medici not to forget that the Florentines retain "the memory of their ancient freedom". In the face of the internal struggles that were tearing Italy apart, it was also a matter of refuting in advance any solution that might come from a foreign prince. Louis XII failed. Neither the Emperor nor the King of Spain could succeed. To conquer a country made up of old republics like the *regnum italicum, you have* to live there. Consequently, what Italy needed to unify it was an Italian prince, and above all not to be annexed to an already established principality such as the Kingdom of Naples.

Republics have a Taste for Freedom

The Virtue
a Prince Needs to Triumph

New principalities can be acquired in two ways: either by *virtue* and one's own weapons, or by the weapons of others and fortune. The opposition seems to be based on a rigorous symmetry, and is immediately doubled (chapters VIII and IX) by a second opposition, that of principalities established by crimes and those instituted thanks to the support of the people, which Machiavelli calls "civil principalities".

Let's start with the principalities studied in chapter VI, those acquired through virtue and its own weapons. First element of reasoning: *virtue*. A new principality is more or less easy to establish or maintain, depending on whether the prince has more or less *virtù*. We can translate *virtù* as "valour", but we can keep the Italian term, which should be understood in its Machiavellian sense of both excellence and virile courage. A prince's *virtù* is not only his valour - for example, his valour in battle, his ability to act without backing down - but also his strategic intelligence and his ability to decide without hesitation what circumstances dictate. *Virtue is* also about intuition: the political leader must see what needs to be done, without necessarily bothering with rigorous reasoning, which is rarely conclusive in human affairs, and ultimately only delays the time for action. Machiavellian virtue is therefore political excellence, and if we want to know what political excellence consists in, we need to learn from history about *virtuoso* princes. Virtue, however, is not the only prerequisite for becoming a prince. In the latter case, however, it is more difficult for the prince to retain his principality.

Among the new princes who acquired their principality by their own valour and arms are "Moses, Cyrus, Romulus, Theseus and others like them" (p. 123). These princes are not adventurers, condottieri or characters like Caesar Borgia. The prince par excellence is a founder and legislator, and if he is not strictly speaking a founder, he can be the one who brings the city back to its principles, to its origins, like Cyrus who "finds the Persians discontented with the domination of the Medes and the Medes softened and effeminate by a long peace" (p. 122). For the latter, fortune plays virtually no role other than to provide an opportunity for the future prince to demonstrate his virtue.

The main difficulty, the one that calls for maximum *virtù*, is that the prince must establish new institutions. And yet: "There is no thing more difficult to undertake, more uncertain to succeed, nor more perilous to conduct than to take the initiative in introducing new institutions. For he who introduces them has for enemies all those who benefit from the old institutions, and he finds lukewarm defenders in those who would benefit from new ones. For this lukewarmness stems partly from the fear of adversaries who have the laws for themselves, and partly from the lack of confidence of men, who have no real confidence in new things unless they have solid experience of them" (p. 123).

To institute new principalities, therefore, you need on the one hand to be a kind of prophet capable of persuading men of the need to introduce a new order, and on the other hand to be armed to force men to continue believing in sermons. We therefore need "armed prophets", as the above-mentioned princes were, for "all armed prophets triumphed, and the unarmed collapsed". The counter-example, that of the unarmed prophet, is Savonarola. "(Saint Augustine, *The City of God*, Book I, preamble, Raulx translation - on the Internet). The reasons for the *fratello*'s rise are the same ones that led to his downfall: he owed his power solely to his prophecies, i.e. his ability to convince the people, the most fragile foundation of political power.

Caesar Borgia,
A Prince with Two Faces

To these new principalities based on the prince's own virtue and weapons, Machiavelli now contrasts those founded on fortune and the weapons of others. These are principalities based "on very changeable and unstable things". But these cases are very rare: indeed, nothing could explain why a simple private individual should become a prince by chance. Chapter VII quickly forks into an examination of the more complex cases of princes who owe their power both to fortune and to their own worth. The two cases cited are that of Francesco Sforza and Caesar Borgia. Machiavelli focuses on the latter, whom he had met some fifteen years before writing *The Prince,* and whose character and methods he had brought to the lordship of Florence in the *Description of the manner employed by the Duke of Valentinois to have Vitellozzo Vitelli, Oliverotto da Fermo, Lord Pagolo and the Duke of Grava-Orsini killed*. This text, which is purely descriptive, makes no value judgment on the Duke of Valentinois and his expeditious methods of disposing of his allies. The lessons to be learned here are that the period during which Caesar Borgia consolidated his power is "worthy of being known and imitated by others" (p. 137). This chapter VII is regarded by anti-Machiavellians as formal proof that the Florentine secretary is an apologist for the worst tyrants. Thus, Jean Bodin declares that Machiavelli, who "elevates to heaven and makes into a paragon of all kings the most disloyal son of a priest who ever lived" (Jean Bodin, preface to the *Six Livres de la République*, 1596, BNF-Gallica), should be considered an "atheist".

An examination of Machiavelli's own words, however, does not support this judgment. In the *Description,* Machiavelli portrayed nothing but cowards and bandits. Caesar Borgia trembles abjectly, and the Florentines' vague promises are enough to comfort him: there's not much *virtù* in there! The Valentinian showed no particular valour: "He was in Imola, full of dread, because, in an instant and contrary to all his thoughts, his soldiers had become his enemies, and he found himself with a nearby war on his hands and no weapons" (p. 374). In short, Caesar Borgia had not foreseen the turn of events, and he found himself without arms. Machiavelli adds that it was the Florentines' proposals that enabled him to regain his courage. In other words, fortune had it that the Florentines' enemies, notably the Vitelli, were also the enemies of Valentinois. But in the face of such a random conjunction of interests, how effective could Borgia's virtue have been? As for the prince's adversaries, they showed a rare pusillanimity, allowing themselves to be caught like little children in the Sinagallia trap set for them by Caesar Borgia. If this episode were to serve as a model for the "new prince" that Machiavelli so obviously called for, and if political virtue could be summed up in this way, then there would be little reason to take an interest in Machiavelli as one of the modern political thinkers whose innovations are of decisive importance.

Understanding Machiavelli's **The Prince**

Let's stick to the text of the *Prince* himself. Caesar Borgia does not belong to the category of virtuous princes who owe their power only to their virtue and their own weapons, those princes who are legislators or refounders (like Romulus or Moses). He owed his power only to his father's fortune, and lost it when his father died. And although he was very valiant and determined, these dispositions did not benefit him, due to an "extraordinary and extreme malignity of fortune" (p. 125). If virtue consists in the ability to turn fortune on its head, we can see that Caesar Borgia ultimately lacked this ability. So he's not so *virtuoso* after all!

In fact, the most notable point in *The Prince* is not the famous Sinagallia trap, but rather the phase that immediately followed. Caesar Borgia's merits can be summed up in a few points. First, he brought order to a country (Romagna) full of "brigandage, dissension and all manner of violence". Secondly, he rid the country of the powerless lords who were holding the people to ransom. Finally, he was ruthless towards his second-in-command, Remirro de Orco, a cruel lord. In this way, he won over the people and, once

Caesar Borgia, A Prince with Two Faces

order was assured, he re-established a civil court in the center of the country (p. 122). The reasons why Borgia's actions deserve to be known and imitated, then, are by no means his cruelty, cunning or lack of scruples, but rather the actions he carried out once he took power, all of which point in the direction of establishing a popular principality. Undoubtedly, Machiavelli was fascinated by the Valentinian's ability to ignore moral scruples in pursuit of his ends, but it is these ends that remain decisive. If the end justifies the means, then the ends must be good. For Machiavelli, a kingdom at peace, a people who no longer have to fear the exactions of the lords, civil courts and a prince who is a friend of the people are all good ends that justify the means employed to achieve them.

Machiavelli notes that the venture soon came to a halt, and that the establishment of strong power did not extend beyond Romagna, as Caesar Borgia had bad luck. His father, Pope Alexander VI, died and he himself fell gravely ill, two events that enabled his enemies to take over the reins of the country and eliminate him. Caesar Borgia had foreseen everything, except that he would find himself almost dying at the moment of his father's death... He is therefore not one of those founding princes who knew how to build a work capable of outliving them. He was not responsible for the accumulation of bad luck that befell him, but Machiavelli would never fail to reproach him for having allowed the election of Cardinal Rovere to the pontificate under the name of Julius II. On this occasion, he showed a lack of foresight that is a lack of virtue in a prince.

Caesar Borgia is not the central model of The *Prince*, as the sequel proves. Chapter VIII deals with "those who reached the principality by crime". There are indeed other ways of attaining power than by *virtue* or fortune, either "by some villainous and abominable means", or by "the favor of his fellow citizens". A villain can become a prince, like Agathocles of Sicily, but only if he demonstrates "energy of mind and body" - in other words, a certain kind of *virtù*... Machiavelli thus notes that energy of mind and body can serve the most evil causes. Moral philosophers usually maintain that crime cannot make the criminal happy, and that ultimately "crime does not pay". A realist, Machiavelli argues, on the contrary, that crime often does pay off: "One might ask how it came about that Agathocles and others like him, after infinite treachery and cruelty, were able to live for a long time in safety in their homeland and defend themselves against their external enemies, and that there was never a conspiracy against him among his fellow citizens, whereas many others were unable to maintain their power through cruelty even in times of peace, to say nothing of the uncertain times of war" (p. 132). The answer to this question is a common-sense one for any student of history: there are two uses of cruelty, one good and one bad. He who must take power by abominable means must calculate his case in such a way that he can commit all the crimes necessary to his domination at the start of his government, so as not to have to repeat them every day, and can instead lavish benefits on his subjects. On the other hand, he who is forced to use violence continuously will never be able to establish a stable rule.

Caesar Borgia, A Prince with Two Faces

Cruelty is a necessary Evil

This chapter VIII seems to legitimize the use of abominable means to conquer power. However, the case deserves to be analyzed in a little more detail. First of all, Machiavelli admits that violence, including the cruellest violence, can be used to seize power, but it cannot be used to exercise it permanently. For a prince who has acquired his principality by these means, only benevolence and civil peace will allow him to last. The ambitious man who wants power for power's sake, and is prepared to do anything to achieve it, must also be rational. In other words, the gratuitous exercise of cruelty in political domination is not only a crime, it's also foolish!

Since men are generally wicked, then men who want to exercise power are wicked too, and probably more inclined than ordinary men to use "wicked" means. We can't expect men in power - any more than any others - to guide their lives according to the Christian principles of love of neighbor and forgiveness of trespasses. We can only hope that they will use their reason sufficiently to limit, in their own interest, the use of lawless violence. Machiavelli says nothing else, and makes no claim to transform human nature, even that of future princes. Machiavellian cynicism is far superior to the sweet illusions of "enlightened despotism", which were widely shared by the philosophers of the Enlightenment, with the exception of Rousseau. Machiavelli presents tyrants as they are, and doesn't believe for a minute that they can become tyrants "with a human face". The distance between the honored monarch and the scoundrel has singularly narrowed. Machiavelli will not be forgiven for this.

When Machiavelli speaks of the crimes of this or that personage, he is not referring to the private conduct of individuals, but to their political action. Once again, history provides numerous examples of conquerors who came to power by violent means, including assassination. But history's judgment

Cruelty is a necessary Evil

rarely takes into account the means, and much more the result. Machiavelli says it openly and clearly. In the history of France, the kings who built up the national unity of this kingdom made up of such diverse populations never shied away from the means. Louis XI maintained himself "in his states" by all manner of crimes and abominable means. Even the "good king" Henry IV never shied away from dissimulation or energetic action when necessary: he could be an interesting example of a Machiavellian prince. It's curious to see that the same people who praise the actions of these great kings show an unmitigated aversion to Machiavelli.

If Caesar Borgia is quoted positively in several places in The *Prince,* it's not because he was a great criminal, but because he knew how to use the means necessary to restore order to the Papal States, and had undertaken to unite divided principalities and republics into a powerful state. Borgia had luck, his father's weapons, *virtue* and a lack of scruples that served him well. Conclusion: he was not the "new prince" Italy needed. And consequently, it is an error of perspective or a lack of attention to reading the work that has led some commentators to make The *Prince the* theory of Caesar Borgia's practice. Machiavelli is neither an apologist for crime nor for the criminal prince.

Chapter IX shows that there is another way to become a prince: "by the favor of his fellow citizens". In the latter case, no exceptional virtue or "total fortune" is required. It's enough to know how to take advantage of the opportunities offered by conflicts between the people, who "desire to be neither commanded nor oppressed by the great ones", and the great ones, who "desire to command and oppress the people". There are therefore two kinds of principalities born of the favor of citizens: those born of the favor of the great and those born of the favor of the people. The former are the most difficult to preserve, since those who made the prince also believe themselves to be his equals, whereas the popular principality is more easily preserved, since hardly anyone in the popular party believes himself to be the prince's equal, and "the aims of the people are more honest than those of the great" (p. 133).

The main constants in Machiavellian thought are that, all other things being equal, the people are better than the great, and whether we're talking about republics or monarchical governments, it's always preferable to rely on the people. This is why Machiavelli, an advocate of freedom, preferred absolute monarchy to a feudal system based on a division of power between the king, *"primus inter pares"* (first among equals), and the feudal lords.

Choose the lesser of Two Evils

The recurring question is whether a prince has the means to defend himself, or whether he must rely on the help of others. This is an essential question, since the freedom of the city or nation is at stake. The first, technical, is that of fortifications and other material means of resisting the attacks of other nations. Thus, speaking of German cities that are well defended, he notes that they are "quite free". The second register is political. It's not enough for a prince to have a solid city; he also needs to avoid being hated. The prince must be courageous, but also wise, i.e. able to win the affection of his people.

What policy should a prince follow if he wants to retain his power? Machiavelli begins by addressing the problem of ecclesiastical principalities. Ecclesiastical principalities are no different from those discussed in the previous chapters. They are acquired like the others, either by *virtue* or by fortune. But they have the particularity that neither *virtù* nor fortune are absolutely necessary to maintain them. "For they are sustained by institutions aged in religion, which have been so powerful and of such quality that they keep their princes in place, no matter how they behave and live. These alone have states and do not defend them, subjects and do not govern them: their states, though undefended, are not taken from them; their subjects, though ungoverned, do not care for them and neither think nor can get rid of them" (p. 137).

Machiavelli obviously has in mind an example of such a principality, the Papal States. The analysis here is highly ambiguous. On the one hand, he implies that the cause that makes these principalities "secure and happy" is to be found in the fact that they are "governed by superior causes": their religious character makes them exceptions that one would have to be very "foolhardy" to talk about. As such, they fall outside the scope of *De principatibus*. Immediately afterwards, however, the author points out that the power of the Papal States remained puny for a very long time, as the other Italian powers managed to keep it relatively impotent. It was only with Alexander VI and Julius II that the Papacy became powerful enough to stand up to the European powers. However, it was not with God's help, but "with money and force" that Alexander VI conquered this power, which the impetuous Julius II perfected. Did the pope's states maintain themselves by force or by their religious character? The question remains open.

Machiavelli is apparently content with a typology of principalities without making value judgments. After all, there are valiant villains who become princes. But implicitly, he orders these various types of principalities with a view to identifying those capable of fulfilling the task set out in chapter XXVI: liberating Italy. The classic distinctions between just and unjust government, or pure and corrupt forms, are set aside, as are the oppositions between law and violence. The ultimate criterion is given in the *Discourses*: "Indeed, we must not condemn those who use violence to restore things, but those who use it to destroy" (p. 209).

Choose the lesser of Two Evils

The example of Caesar Borgia, so extreme, so debatable, so abominable even, shows precisely where the dividing line lies. As for republics, Machiavelli obviously prefers them - and among principalities, he shows that the best are precisely those that are closest to a republic - but, in the *Prince*'s context, there are no republics left in Italy, all of them are corrupt (including his beloved Florence, which has just surrendered to the Medici), and it's the emergency that must be faced.

Only "Armed Prophets" Triumph

The military question cannot be separated from that of political institutions. For a state to survive, it needs "good laws and good weapons", "because there can be no good laws where there are no good weapons, and where there are good weapons, there must be good laws" (p. 139).

The link between laws and weapons is so indissoluble that Machiavelli refrains from talking about laws, concentrating instead on the question of weapons. The formulation of this relationship between weapons and laws is not entirely clear, however. The first part is easily understood: if there are no good weapons, it's because the laws have not provided for the defense of the state, and therefore the laws are no good. But the second part of the sentence is not symmetrical with the first.

Where there are good weapons, "there must" be good laws. So it could be that a state has bad laws, yet is well-equipped to defend itself. Machiavelli leaves this question in the dark. We must assume that, since the defense of the city is the defense of the freedom of the state, this implies that the state itself, in its internal constitution, must guarantee the freedom of its citizens in order to be worth defending. Note again that principalities must have good laws, and this distinguishes a prince from a tyrant.

The prince's weapons must be "his own", as "mercenaries and auxiliaries" are useless and dangerous. The indictment of mercenary armies is unmitigated. "For they are disunited, ambitious, without discipline, disloyal: valiant among friends, cowardly among enemies; without fear of God and without faith with men; and one defers one's fall only so long as one defers the assault; during peace you are robbed by them, during war by enemies" (p. 139).

Machiavelli speaks from experience, as chancellor of the seigniory who, from the outset, called for Florence to have its own arms, as commissioner of the armies during the siege of Pisa, as organizer of the militia and as defender of the city walls. He was also an Italian patriot who saw Charles VIII "take Italy with his chalk" (p. 140). Ancient history confirms this experience: Rome and Sparta remained free as long as they were armed. The example of Rome helps us to understand the meaning Machiavelli gives to the relationship between good arms and good laws. The citizens of the republic are free because they defend themselves and have no professional army. It is also for this reason that they are free citizens within the republic: the "great" cannot act without the agreement of those who make up the city's armed force, as the episode of that veritable "strike with the armies" that was the secession of the Roman plebs on Mount Aventine powerfully demonstrated. Conversely, in the imperial era, the Romans entrusted their defense to others, in particular to armies composed of the peoples that Rome had enslaved, while the Roman citizen was content to squander the riches that conquests brought him. In the process, however, the people gradually lost their own freedom and came under the domination of the armies that were supposed to defend them.

What applies to mercenary armies also applies to auxiliary armies. The example of Caesar Borgia confirms this overall judgment. Borgia began his conquest of Romagna with auxiliary armies, then took mercenaries into his service and finally built his own army, and "he was never held in high esteem, except when everyone saw that he had full possession of his arms" (p. 144). More general conclusion: "In short, other people's weapons either fall from your shoulders, or weigh you down, or squeeze you" (p. 145).

That's why war and military institutions and discipline are the prince's proper profession. It's the "only profession suited to those in command". But command requires practical intellectual training. It requires knowledge of geography - geography is for making war, as Yves Lacoste would say - and of history, the meditation on which constitutes the elementary education of the prince's profession. But it is above all moral training, i.e. learning how to conduct oneself in order to acquire and retain power, that the prince needs most.

Only "Armed Prophets" Triumph

Don't confuse Moral Virtue with Political Virtue

Let's move on to an examination of the *Prince*'s most "sulphurous" chapters, those in which Machiavelli's alleged immoralism is given free rein, those in which the separation between morality and politics is pushed to its supreme point. But to understand the importance of what follows, we need to be on the right ground. Political action and morality do not mix, as we know well enough, and Machiavelli would hardly be breaking new ground. But Machiavelli's strength, or intolerability, lies precisely in not disguising the conflict, not trying to resolve it by purely verbal means. Referring to the radical means to be employed by any newly established prince, Machiavelli, in the *Discourses*, concludes: "These are very cruel means and contrary to all the rules of life, not only Christian but human; every man must flee from them and prefer the condition of simple private individual to that of king, at the price of the destruction of so many men. Nevertheless, anyone who has rejected the path of good must follow that of evil in order to maintain himself. But most men choose certain middle paths, which are the worst of all, because they do not know how to be either completely good or completely evil [...]" (p. 238).

Speaking of the surrender of the lord of Perugia, Giovanpagolo, to Julius II, Machiavelli remarked that, unable to be perfectly good, one must know how to be honorably bad. No serious historian, no honest politician could contradict Machiavelli on this point. Machiavelli's originality certainly does not lie in distinguishing between morality and politics, nor in admitting that the exercise of power requires the use of extraordinary means that everyday morality rejects. That princes are not subject to common law is a banality in a society as hierarchical as medieval. Augustine's readers know that evil princes are merely God's instrument for persuading us that earthly life is miserable and hopeless. To focus on Machiavelli's moralism or immoralism is to make a radical mistake. Machiavelli is no bigot - to say the least... However, there is no systematic charge against morality in general, and Christian morality in particular. On the contrary, moral values are a necessary component of those civic virtues that enable *vivere civile* (civil life), whose disappearance (in licentiousness) signals the corruption of the people and heralds the ruin of the state. Political action itself is not devoid of values. The end justifies the means, but only if the end is praiseworthy, and the praiseworthy end par excellence is political order, which enables us to live in peace.

To understand the specificity of The *Prince*, we need to read chapter XV in detail. The purpose is clearly stated: "Since my intention is to write things that are useful to those who listen to them, it seemed more relevant to me to follow the actual truth of things than the idea one has of them" (p. 148). If we're talking about political power, then, there are two planes: "effective truth" and imagination. The pamphlet's first objective, then, is to dismantle the processes of imagination in order to arrive at *verità effettuale della cosa* (effective truth *of* the thing). Let's recall the dedication: it announces that the aim is to look at princes from the point of view of the people, for "to know the nature of the people well, one must be a prince, and to know the nature of princes well, one must be of the people" (p. 110). The conjunction of this dedication and chapter XV seems to vindicate Rousseau's judgment quoted above: "By pretending to give lessons to kings, he has given great lessons to the people. Machiavelli's *Prince* is the book of republicans."

To leave it at that would be to interpret Machiavelli as the first great demystifier - a possible interpretation, but one that is really too one-sided. For Machiavelli's aim is to reflect on the conditions under which stable government can be established, and thus to think about power structures. Indeed: "Many have imagined republics and principalities which have never been seen or known to exist. For there is so much distance between the way one lives and the way one ought to live, that he who leaves what one does for what one ought to do, learns rather to lose himself than to preserve himself: for a man who wants in all matters to make a profession of goodness, he must fall down in the midst of people who are not good" (p. 148). The demystifier denounces: power wants to be moral, but its moralism is only the hypocritical mask of cruelty and *libido dominandi* (the desire to dominate), and so we must either denounce all power as immoral, or want power founded on divine law, as that "disarmed prophet", Friar Savonarola, wanted. But this is not Machiavelli's point. The absence of government is unthinkable: governments are human institutions that men naturally need to protect themselves. What's more, a good prince in the midst of bad men is doomed to collapse. What's needed, then, is a power capable of ordering the city, and capable, depending on the circumstances, of employing morally good or morally bad means. And to achieve this, we need to start from "true things", not imagined things.

Starting from the truth means understanding how the relationship between ruler and ruled works, or, if we prefer, staying more strictly within the framework of the "opuscule", the relationship between the prince and his subjects. Machiavelli places the subjects' judgment of the prince at the forefront of this relationship: "Princes, because they are higher up, are judged according to the qualities that bring them blame or praise. That is to say, one is judged liberal, the other cowardly [...], one is judged generous, the other rapacious, one cruel, the other merciful [...]" (p. 148).

The long enumeration of vices and virtues leads to a triple observation:

1. We'd love a prince to have all the qualities we consider good, but it's impossible for a man to have them all; and besides, if he had them all, he'd fall apart, a perfectly good man in the midst of generally bad men.

2. In any case, a prince, in order to govern, cannot observe them all; there are vices necessary to exercise power.

3. Nevertheless, the prince must take care of his reputation, which is his main asset for governing.

Unveiling the secret and the "doublethink" is what guides the examination of the virtues for which the prince is renowned. Thus, "it is good to be held as generous", but Machiavelli immediately adds: "Nevertheless, liberality practiced to the point of having a reputation for it, harms you; for if it is practiced virtuously and as it should be practiced, it is not known and you do not lose the bad reputation of its opposite" (p. 149). Indeed, ostentatious virtue is not virtue. Charity that shows itself is not charitable, but pure vanity (an operation of communication, we would say today!) and so the good man is the one who practices liberality without showing it, whereas the prince must, on the contrary, show it, and so, even if he really does practice liberality, it is already no longer a meritorious virtue. But there's more: the practice of liberality can also be harmful, because it must always meet its limits, and by giving limits to his liberality, the prince incurs the name of ladre. Finally, "a prince must therefore, if he is wise, not worry about the name of ladre" (p. 150). Finally, to be ladre for a prince is not the same as for a private individual. The prince must not mind incurring the reproach of ladrerie, for he is not stingy with his own money but with public money, and is therefore concerned not to have to steal from his subjects. And if this reproach of ladrerie is in itself an evil, it is only a lesser evil. Indeed, the overly liberal prince generally ends up emptying the coffers, and is forced to find money by any means necessary: "Among all the things a prince must guard against, there is the fact of being contemptible and odious: liberality leads you to both of these things. So it is wiser to keep the name of ladre, which engenders a bad reputation devoid of hatred, than to be forced, for wanting to be generous, to incur the name of rapacious, which engenders a bad reputation accompanied by hatred" (p. 150-151).

Complete inversion of values: what is a virtue in a private person (generosity) becomes a vice by becoming public, and conversely, the vice of the laird as a private person is a public virtue. There is no trace of Machiavellian "immoralism" in this chapter. The demands of the public good determine behavior other than that of private salvation. But if the morality of an action or behavior depends on the value of the ends it serves, we can see that it is just as moral for a private individual to be generous as for a prince not to be! And in the former case, there is none of the "reversal of moral values" of which the Florentine secretary is so often accused or credited.

The same reasoning is applied to the question of whether it is better for a prince to be loved than feared. A good reputation would require a prince to be merciful: "Nevertheless, he must take care not to misuse mercy. Caesar Borgia was considered cruel; nevertheless, his cruelty had restored Romagna, unified it, and brought it back to peace and confidence. In which, if we consider carefully, we will see that he was far more merciful than the Florentine people who, to escape the name of cruelty, let Pistoia be destroyed" (p. 151).

The politician is not a moralist in the bedroom, advocating abstract rules without regard for their consequences. Machiavelli, on the contrary, defines morality by calculating consequences. All in all, he asserts, the cruelty of the Valentinians caused less misfortune and brought about more happy reforms than the pity of the Florentines. Once again, not immoralism, but a certain kind of moral reasoning. Who is more moral, the one who refuses to bear arms against the tyrant in the name of biblical precept, or the one who risks his life and saves the innocent? The one who refuses all violence or the one who, if necessary through violence, protects peace and security? Consequently, the new prince must not "shun the name of cruel". But Machiavelli adds: "Nevertheless, the prince must be balanced in his opinions and decisions, and not frighten himself, proceeding in a manner tempered by wisdom and humanity, so that excessive confidence does not make him imprudent, and too much distrust does not make him unbearable" (p. 151).

It's almost a moral middle ground. But it still has to fit in with the necessities of power. The ideal would be to balance humanity with the ability to make cruel decisions. But this ideal is probably out of reach, as men "are generally ungrateful, changeable, simulators and dissimulators, cowards in the face of danger, greedy for profit" (p. 152). For this reason, we can hardly hope to obtain obedience through love, and so it is better to be feared, taking care not to transform this fear into hatred.

For Machiavelli, reason is rarely active, and its own forces are powerless to govern men. Rather, men are governed by their passions, and so the precepts to be followed by those who wish to govern are to be found in the balance of the "humours". The virtues attributed to the prince are only as important as the effect they have on the imagination of his subjects. Cruelty provokes fear, that is to say, to use Spinoza's expression, a "sadness" linked to the inconstant imagination of something dubious. This ambivalence lies at the heart of Machiavellian thinking. The prince, and rulers in general, must inspire fear in the masses, but must act to avoid having to fear their hatred.

Half Man, Half Beast

In Greek mythology, the centaur Chiron, half-man, half-horse, is the teacher in essence. His disciples include Asclepius, the god of medicine, and Achilles, to whom he taught music, medicine and the arts of war. It is from Chiron that the new prince must learn, since, as we have just seen, he will need to know medicine, the art of regulating the humours, as well as the art of war. Machiavelli makes a very particular use of the myth of Chiron: the prince must be like Chiron, half-man and half-beast. Indeed, as Machiavelli says, there are two ways of fighting: "One with laws, the other with force; the first is proper to man, the second to beasts" (p. 153). Now, to govern men, the first way is not enough, and so "a prince must know how to use both man and beast". But the beast here is still a double animal: the prince must use the lion and the fox, "for the lion does not defend itself from traps and the fox does not defend itself from wolves" (p. 154). Reason (laws) is not enough to govern - that's been said enough - but neither is force. To this must be added cunning to outwit traps, and this is why, as a good fox, the prince must be able to deceive: "Consequently, a wise sovereign cannot and must not keep his word when such behavior risks turning against him, and when the reasons for committing it have disappeared" (p. 154).

An assertion to be counted among those that have done so much to build the bad reputation of the author of The *Prince*. It's a common-sense assertion, confirmed by historical experience. We could give "an infinite number of modern examples". No great power has been built without making the Machiavellian precept its golden rule. And there is no need to go back to Alexander Borgia for this... There is no hero of national historiography who has not displayed his fox-like qualities, and none who has neglected the following advice: "But it is necessary to know how to disguise this nature well and to

Half Man, Half Beast

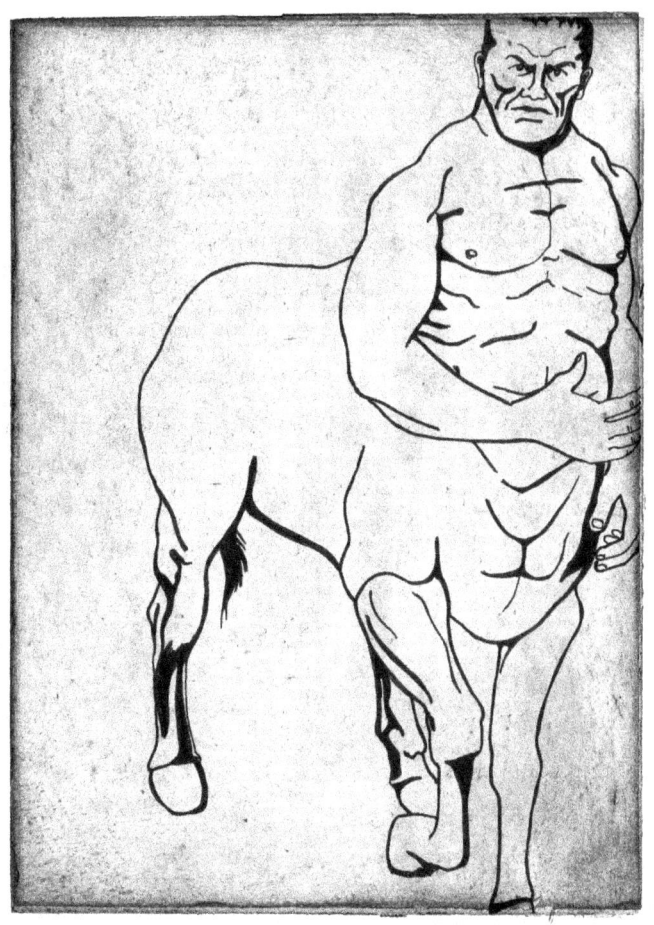

be a simulator and dissimulator: men are so simple and obey present necessities so well that he who deceives will always find someone who will allow himself to be deceived" (p. 154).

In this task of simulation and dissimulation, princes generally find the more or less benevolent help of moralists and other propagandists who are highly skilled at disguising foxes as lions. There's an interesting shift here: princes are obliged not to allow themselves to become entangled in the precepts of ordinary morality, because men are simulators and dissimulators (p. 152). But now it's the princes who are simulators and dissimulators, and find opposite them men simple enough to want to be deceived! General wickedness is not so great that it cannot be contained by the skilful action of a *virtuoso* prince.

Machiavelli does not support this view of man as a wolf to man. The prince-lion must know how to fight the wolves, but not all wolves are men: many are "simple" and preoccupied with everyday necessities. The wolves the prince must guard against are more likely to be the "great ones" who are ready to take his place, with whom he must make agreements, but of whom he must never be a prisoner.

Chiron not only had to teach the prince the arts of war, music and medicine. The theatrical arts undoubtedly have an even greater place. Disguising oneself, giving a false impression, appearing sometimes under the fur of a lion, sometimes under that of a fox - these are the techniques of the prince. Machiavelli sees politics first and foremost as a theatrical staging designed to fascinate the multitude enough to make them accept obedience. And it is only because he knows this art of staging that the prince can follow the Machiavellian precept: "For a prince, therefore, it is not necessary to have all the above-mentioned virtues, but it is quite necessary to appear to have them. I dare say this: if you have them and always observe them, they are harmful; if you appear to have them, they are useful" (p. 154).

Let's take another look at the misconception of those who make the discussion of the *Prince*'s immoralism the central issue. With this razor-sharp style, the aim is to dismantle the machine of power

- the machine as theatrical machinery - in order to rebuild another, even as the old one lies shattered in the disasters of *povera Italia*.

Keeping up Appearances: The Art of Governing is an Art of Communication

Machiavelli's supposed immoralism is in reality nothing more than the absence of a transcendent morality that would rise above the contingencies of human existence. There is a Machiavellian morality that has been difficult to perceive, because it does not refer to the concern each individual should have for his own soul, but only to the practical conditions of living together in a well-ordered state. For the prince, then, it's not a question of being good or bad, but of governing in such a way as to maintain the order of the state, in other words, to last. And to do this, one must "be able and know how to change completely". And so the prince must "not deviate from good if he can, but know how to enter evil when forced to do so". The key, however, lies in the ability to keep up appearances: "A prince must therefore take great care never to let anything come out of his mouth that is not full of the five qualities named above, and to appear to him, to be seen and heard, all mercy, all good faith, all righteousness, all humanity, all religion. And there is nothing more necessary to appear than this last quality" (p. 155).

These appearances make it possible to govern the many. In this field, the means are always judged by the success, and we must obviously guard against judging political leaders by their professions of faith: "Certain prince of the present time, whom it is not good to name, never preaches anything other than peace and good faith, and he is the greatest enemy of both; both, if he had observed them, would several times have deprived him of his credit and his power" (p. 155). Clearly, it is impossible to govern by violence alone. It also requires what we might call "ideology", i.e. the ability to make people mistake flattering appearances for reality. But this is precisely where an interesting twist occurs. Machiavelli has no use for the intentions of the new prince. Bad politics is made out of good feelings. But the desire to keep up appearances - those appearances that are the reality of power - determines a number of political behaviors that are imperative for any prince wishing to conquer and retain power. For example, he must "shun contempt and hatred". A formidable logic of appearance: if the prince can only govern because he "will always find someone who will let himself be deceived", if he governs by playing on the imagination of his subjects, it is, conversely, the gaze of these same subjects that becomes the main force of reaction. This gaze of the subjects becomes the prince's law. And so, after admitting that the prince can use evil to achieve his ends, Machiavelli defines imperative rules for these same ends, whose strict observance will prevent the prince from making himself odious or despicable. The prince may be a coward, but he cannot be rapacious, that is, "usurp the property and women of his subjects". Honor and property are therefore inalienable assets of subjects. Those who accuse Machiavelli of being some kind of inventor of totalitarianism should have meditated on this passage, which is all the more interesting in that this clause defines the "rights" of the subject that all political power must respect, on pain of being odious and deserving of what happens to odious governments. We might think here of Locke, who asserts that political power can dispose of citizens' lives when it comes to war, but not of their property. The prince must also shun contempt, which is engendered by weakness, pusillanimity, the inability to resolutely carry out decided actions, and so on. Machiavelli calls for something that anyone who thinks seriously about politics will demand: that the political orientation and decisions of power are always clearly expressed, and rigorously conducted. Courage, gravity, firmness: these are the qualities the new prince must demonstrate. As we can see, the vocabulary of morality, which had been reduced to an appearance - it is more useful to show virtues than to actually possess them - makes a strong comeback in these final chapters of The *Prince*.

These moral virtues are put at the service of a political strategy: have good weapons to have good friends. Machiavelli leads a rather long discussion on conspiracies, which ends as follows: "I conclude, therefore, that a prince must take little account of conspiracies if the people are fond of him; but if they are hostile to him and hate him, he must fear everything and everyone. Well-ordered states and wise princes have carefully thought out how not to drive the great into despair, how to satisfy the people and keep them happy; for this is one of the most important problems a prince encounters" (p. 157).

The People must be Satisfied

The prince's strategy is therefore quite straightforward: to solve "one of the most important problems", that of satisfying the people without excessively burdening the great, in other words, to govern while respecting the balance of moods so characteristic of the republic. So, while there is a major difference between a republican government and a principality, the problems to be solved are fundamentally the same, and the dynamics of social forces are no different. The new prince called by Machiavelli is a kind of "democratic dictator". Significantly, Machiavelli illustrates this good princely government with the example of France, a kingdom with many good institutions, particularly parliaments, to curb the hubris and ambitions of the great. This is a "third judge charged with the task of striking down the great and favoring the small without prejudice to the king" (p. 157). Whether parliaments really had this function historically is open to debate, but this example is clearly decisive in understanding Machiavelli's work: far from being purely arbitrary, princely government, when it is at its most secure and well-ordered, is already what we might call a "rule of law", since power relations in society are regulated by a "third judge".

The prince's "democratic" character is also underlined when it comes to defense issues. While Machiavelli is wary of taking overly clear-cut general positions, as the decisions to be taken would have to be discussed on a case-by-case basis, he still supports the need for the new prince to arm his subjects: to have arms of one's own is to have the arms of one's people. As for other technical issues - such as the role of fortresses - these are, after all, relatively minor matters. Without expressing an opinion on the necessity of fortresses, the future provender of the walls of Florence concludes: "I will blame anyone who, relying on fortresses, does not care to be hated by the people" (p. 166).

Chapters XXI, XXII and XXIII develop some of the ways to avoid being hated by the people and to win their esteem. Power techniques and moral virtues are closely interwoven. For example, the prince must be able to make people talk about him, through external adventures in which he imposes his courage, his glory, his decision-making ability, and, through a policy of "communication", as we would say today, the prince must make people speak well of him whenever possible: "strive to give of himself in all actions a reputation as a great man and of exceptional intelligence" (p. 167). But it's not just a question of propaganda and staging. You also need to demonstrate genuine qualities, such as knowing how to "be a true friend or a true foe" - in other words, how not to dissimulate! It also requires prudence, particularly in alliances, knowing how to surround oneself properly and avoiding flatterers.

What perhaps complicates the understanding of Machiavelli's thought is this constant mixture of simple pragmatic maxims and moral virtues. But in reality, there is no such mixture, since the moral virtues are just as pragmatic as the pragmatic maxims, insofar as their value lies solely in the advantage they give to the prince. But conversely, all these pragmatic maxims of Machiavelli's "cold realism", or even "cynicism", are in fact moral, since morality is first and foremost the quest for the best possible civil life, which can only be achieved with a well-ordered and therefore stable state.

Necessary Evil

Machiavelli is said to be the theorist of raison d'État, a system of political justification for acts that are morally unacceptable but useful for the defense of the state and, by the same token, useful for the community that the state is charged with defending. Nowadays, raison d'État gets a bad press, probably with good reason, and, as a result, "Machiavellianism" continues to bear the stigma. In this case, it is necessary to examine two distinct questions. Firstly, are we really right to condemn raison d'état almost unconditionally? And secondly, which of Machiavelli's political and theoretical positions deserve to be classified under the heading of "raison d'État"?

Indeed, it's a rather curious accusation. Firstly, because raison d'État is a universal fact, and all states are "Machiavellian". As far as we know, no state renounces the use of violence, whether at home or abroad. With the exception of a few small states such as the Republic of San Marino, all states have an army and a police force that have a monopoly on the exercise of legitimate violence, to use Max Weber's expression. Even states that have abolished the death penalty give themselves the right to kill in war operations - even if they are usually careful to cover these operations with the mantle of "defense of democracy" or "Western values". State secrecy is essential to maintain the state in the face of its internal or external enemies, and with state secrecy come spies, undercover agents, bribing officials in other countries, or snitches in opposition parties or groups rightly or wrongly described as "subversive". Deceiving the enemy in wartime, or not revealing one's full intentions in peacetime, are qualities for leaders, whereas deception is considered a sin or a punishable offence when it comes to affairs between private individuals.

One might imagine, however, that recourse to these procedures dictated by *raison d'État* would have to be banned by a truly democratic government, or one that set itself the goal not of maintaining a social order based on domination, but of abolishing it. It is to be feared, however, that this is no more than a sweet reverie, condemned to remain a reverie. If we believe that political organization is necessary to enable people to live together, if we refuse to believe that the anarchist ideal is possible, then we have to admit that people are contained by law, by force and by trickery. The rule of law is certainly better than the absence of laws, but it's also partly a disguise, one of those ideas that strikes the imagination, an idea that works quite well because you can always find people to be fooled. But in the "rule of law", there are police truncheons and guns, prisons and prison guards, state secrecy, the "confidential defense" document, archives banned for fifty years, etc., all of which bear witness to the fact that men are governed not only by means peculiar to men, but also by means peculiar to beasts. Perhaps we can only hope that the government will use all the instruments at its disposal wisely, and that the people, sufficiently enamored of their own freedom, will not let it abuse power.

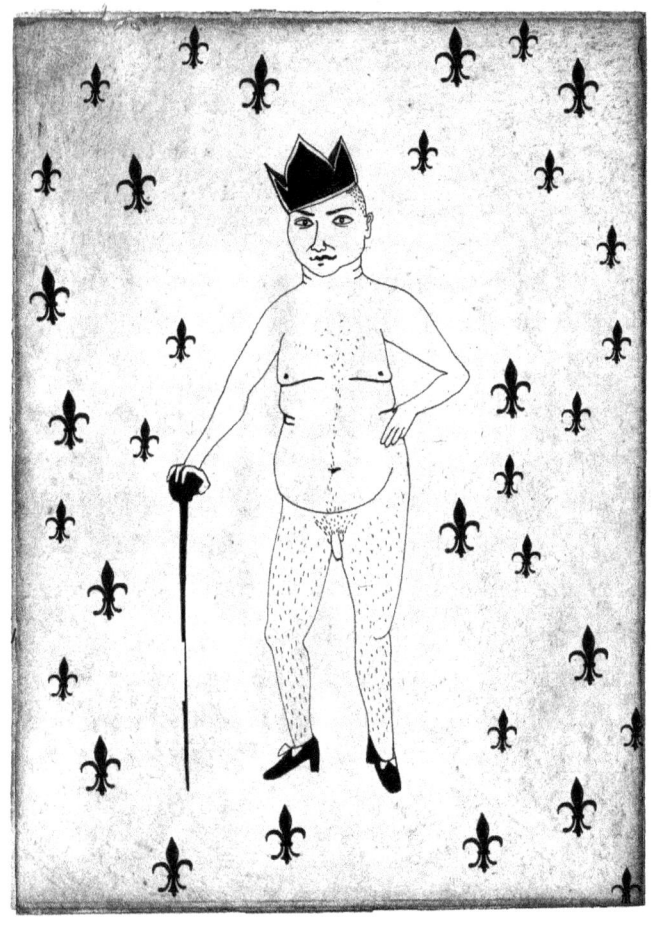

But as long as there are reasons for the existence of the state, there is "raison d'État".

Machiavelli committed a major crime, however: instead of cloaking state violence in the moralistic denials with which it is usually associated, he called it by its proper name. In Machiavelli's texts, there is no such thing as cunning or dissimulation. He goes straight to the "actual truth of things". There's nothing less Machiavellian than Machiavelli's works! Against the mystifications of power, Machiavelli's dismantling of state machinery aims to say to every reader, to every citizen perhaps: this is what this mechanism is; this is how and why you obey.

History Proves the Victors Right

It's also worth clarifying what Machiavelli explicitly defends, which could be classified under the heading *"raison d'État"*. He does not support just any form of political power. There are criminal regimes (chapter VIII) that clearly do not fall into the category of the new princes we are going to urge to liberate Italy from the barbarians. We have also seen that the prince must avoid the hatred of the people. He makes himself feared by striking the imagination and being ruthless when necessary, but he himself is always under the fear of the people. Even the brilliant deeds by which a monarch establishes his glory and empire are not always to be praised. When Ferdinand of Aragon attacks the Jews, Machiavelli's grating irony is heard: "He decided on a pious cruelty in driving out and stripping his kingdom of the Marranos: there can be no more pitiful and exceptional example" (p. 166).

Once again, the question is how to distinguish the founding of a republic or kingdom from that of a tyranny. Thus, addressing the murder of Remus by his brother Romulus, Machiavelli writes in the *Discourses*: "A wise mind will never reproach someone for having performed an extraordinary action to organize a kingdom or create a republic. If the facts accuse him, the effects must excuse him. When they are good, as in the case of Romulus, they always excuse him" (*Discourse on the First Decade of Titus Livius*, p. 209). Romulus's "extraordinary" action was carried out for the common good, not for his own benefit; this is the only criterion for distinguishing legitimate from illegitimate actions. This distinction is, moreover, an extremely classic one: what distinguishes just from unjust government is the interest of those who govern. A single man who governs for the common good is a monarch, and if he governs solely for his own interests, then he is a tyrant.

Our repulsion at the justification of "raison d'État" is rooted in this distinction, and could therefore serve as a reasonable basis for it. When rulers keep certain actions secret, or protect behaviour that would otherwise be considered criminal, they are not criticized if their actions have ends that are generally considered legitimate. To take contemporary examples, it is worth noting that public opinion was hardly moved by the not always very orthodox methods used by General de Gaulle's government to get rid of the OAS. On the other hand, when the same actions are supposed to serve only the interests of those in power - for example, if secrecy is imposed to cover up the errors or faults of a particular senior official - then these actions are condemnable, and the invocation of the raison d'État appears to be no more than a pitiful excuse for the inexcusable.

The Ultimate Goal: To Liberate the Nation

The final pages of The *Prince* give the full meaning of the work. Caesar Borgia is praised for having attempted to reconstitute a viable state, and for having brought to heel, by the hard way, the "greats" and other warlords who were decimating the region. But what *The Prince is about is* something quite different, a historic task that would not be accomplished until almost four centuries later.

The question of Italian unity, in fact, dominates Machiavelli's thinking, as can be seen from the beginning of his *History of Florence*. Italy is not a state, but a nation, historically rooted in the formation and development of Roman domination over the peninsula. The apparent opposition between *The Prince* and the *Discourses on the First Decade of*

Titus Livius finds its solution if we consider that *The Prince* is not a manual of political cynicism or a second-degree denunciation of political power, but an attempt to find a solution to the question of Italian unity. The crises of the republics and their inability to unite their efforts to ensure their freedom from foreign influence are indisputable. Machiavelli was well aware that each city played its own game, and he had a lucid vision of his Florentine homeland. The "princes of Italy lost their states" through a lack of courage, an inability to understand the need for arms, an inability to bond with the people. As we saw above, fortune, which has great power over human affairs, is not to blame, but can be resisted.

A new prince is needed, one who is "wise and valiant", because in Italy there is a need to "introduce a form that will bring honor and good to all the men of this country" (p. 176). The prince is an introducer of form, a reformer, the one who reforms the nation, but also the one who, like the religious reformer, brings it back to its primitive principles when they have been forgotten. The first example given to illustrate what we're talking about is a revea-

The Ultimate Goal: To Liberate the Nation

ling one: Moses. Machiavelli's contemporary Italy was more enslaved than the Hebrews, so it needed a Moses to give it the courage to rise up and fight, and also to give it laws. Hegel, a penetrating reader of Machiavelli, could not fail to find something of great interest in this aspect of Machiavelli's thought, for he starts from a rather similar observation: France, Spain and England have formed powerful national states, but Hegel's Germany is like Machiavelli's Italy, divided and now the theater where foreign powers clash. Quoting at length from the last chapter of The *Prince,* Hegel writes: "To a man who expresses himself with such gravity, no baseness of heart or lightness of mind can be attributed" (*The Constitution of Germany*, in *Écrits politiques*, translated from the German by Michel Jacob, Éditions Champ Libre, 1977, p. 118).

After criticizing the disapproval that public opinion attaches to Machiavelli's name, Hegel continues: "Machiavelli's goal of elevating Italy to statehood is already misunderstood by all those blind people who see in this author's work only a justification for tyranny and a golden mirror for an ambitious despot. But even when this goal is recognized, it is the means, it is said, that are detestable, and here morality has plenty of time to spout its platitudes, such as that the end does not justify the means, etc. But there can be no question here of the choice of means: gangrenous limbs cannot be cured with lavender water; a state in which poison and murder have become common weapons admits of nothing but energetic remedies; after a period of corruption, life can only be reorganized by force and constraint" (*loc. cit.*).

Defending a book - *The Prince* - that expresses "a conception full of grandeur and truth", Hegel goes on the offensive: "It would not be useless to say a few words here about aspects that are generally forgotten, i.e., the other quite ideal conditions that Machiavelli demands of a perfect prince and that none has fulfilled since, not even the one who refuted him." (*loc.cit.*) Hegel is referring to Frederick II, author of an "anti-Machiavelli". To say that Machiavelli's voice went unheard is perhaps a bit hasty: it had many important philosophical echoes. But if we're talking about those who deal with political matters,

Hegel's assertion is undoubtedly justified, at least until the 19th century. It was in his homeland that the Florentine secretary would once again be heard, at a time when the question of national unity would once again be posed and resolved.

Why does the republican Machiavelli take on the Persona of the Prince?

What does the *Prince* mean? We can begin to pinpoint it. In his study of *Italian Democracies*, Julien Luchaire made this pertinent observation: "Machiavelli's statism rests on a democratism, the sincerity of which can scarcely be suspected. The *Prince* himself does not deny it: for Machiavelli's prince is not the representative of a sovereign family concentrating all the powers of the state. He is the State embodied in an individual" (*Les Démocraties italiennes*, Flammarion, 1920, p. 296). Gramsci is responsible for some of the most penetrating considerations on the profound meaning of the *Prince*. In the *Cahiers de Prison (Prison Notebooks)*, Machiavelli's name recurs several times, particularly in the relatively extensive notes in the thirteenth notebook:

"The fundamental character of The *Prince* is that it is not a systematic treatise but a 'living' book, in which political ideology and political science merge in the dramatic form of 'myth'" (*Quaderni del carcere*, Einaudi, 2007, p. 1555). The term "myth" is obviously not secondary. Gramsci refers to Georges Sorel. In his critical report on Marxism, Sorel highlights the importance of myths in revolutionary politics. Discussing the importance of religious ideologies in past revolutions, Sorel criticizes Engels. Against Engels' idea that it is only in the early phases of the bourgeois revolution that there is a correlation between social revolution and ideologies elaborated in theological form, Sorel writes in his *Matériaux d'une théorie du prolétariat*: "It is a question of knowing what myths have, in the various epochs, impelled the overthrow of existing situations; ideologies have been no more than translations of these myths in abstract forms" (*Matériaux d'une théorie du prolétariat (1918)*, UQAC, "Classiques des sciences sociales", digital edition, 2003, p. 178).

In Sorel's thinking, myths are the real engines of social transformation. If utopian socialists remained small groups with no real lasting social influence, this was due to their lack of myths: "The utopians did not succeed in determining serious movements in the world, because they did not have at their disposal myths endowed with the driving power that would have been necessary" (*ibid.*, p. 180). What Sorel interprets as Marx's catastrophism, the idea that the capitalist mode of production is going to its doom in a kind of final crisis that will pave the way for social transformation, is one of those myths that Sorel parallels with the great anarcho-syndicalist myth of the general strike. In his *Reflections on Violence*, he continues this theory of myths, showing that these beliefs that reasonable minds find chimerical often have a fundamental role in history. Thus: "The first Christians expected the return of Christ and the total ruin of the pagan world, with the establishment of the kingdom of the saints at the end of the first generation. The catastrophe did not occur, but Christian thought made such use of the apocalyptic myth that some contemporary scholars would have us believe that the whole of Jesus' preaching focused on this single subject"

(*Réflexions sur la violence (1912)*, Marcel Rivière, 1936, p. 177-178).

Machiavelli, through the new prince, personifies, in an anthropomorphic way, says Gramsci, a collective will that he calls for. This is why "the *Prince* could be studied as an example of a Sorellian myth" (Gramsci, *op. cit.*, p. 1555). Why does the republican Machiavelli use the figure of the prince to transform the political program of a new state into a veritable myth? First of all, let's note that the prince is not a hereditary prince, but a new prince, i.e. someone who has become a prince either through his own arms (revolutionaries!), or with the consent of his fellow citizens (in civil principalities). These new princes are classic figures in the history of medieval and renaissance Italy. They were either princes more or less legally born of the communes, or condottieri who became rulers of the city that employed them. Examples of the former include the Viscontis, "lords" (i.e., members of the commune's governing body, the seigniory) who ruled from the time of John Galeas under the name of "Duke of Milan", or the Medici. Of the latter, we might mention Francesco

Sforza, who, after serving as a condottiere in the service of Milan, took the city by storm in 1450, and of course the Valentinois, Duke of Romagna.

For Machiavelli, none of these figures is an example to follow, including Valentinois. So the new prince is none of them. But these figures are those of courageous, determined men, ready to do whatever it takes to acquire and retain their states. So, by embodying the new state to be built in the figure of the prince, Machiavelli constructs a myth, and like all myths it must borrow its visible elements from a historical reality, transfigured as is that of the condottiere Guidoriccio da Fogliano in Simone Martini's fresco in Siena's Palazzo Pubblico. But we can only agree with Gramsci's judgment: "The utopian character of The *Prince* lies in the fact that 'the prince' did not exist in historical reality, he did not present himself to the Italian people with characters of objective immediacy, but was a pure doctrinal abstraction, the symbol of the leader, of the ideal condottiere; but the passionate, mythical elements, contained in the entire brief volume, with a dramatic movement of great effect, are taken up

Understanding Machiavelli's The Prince

and become alive in the conclusion, in the invocation of a 'really existing' prince" (Gramsci, *op. cit*, p. 1556).

This is why, according to Gramsci, the last chapter, the exhortation to liberate Italy from the barbarians, is not something extrinsic but what gives meaning to the work, what makes it a "political manifesto". There is indeed a combination of cold logic and imagination in *The Prince*, which explains the shift from the first twenty-four chapters to the last two: the first twenty-four chapters are descriptive, cold, with a hint of bitter irony always piercing through; the last two, chapter XXV on fortune that can be forced, and the exhortation in chapter XXVI, call for action and combat. This shift in register confirms that the new prince is indeed a myth, but one that makes explicit the "norms of salvation".

Conclusion:
Against Moralistic Preaching,
A Political Thought for Today

Enough has been said. Machiavelli is a moralist and a master of political science. The actual truth of the matter must be known to anyone who asks the question of political action. The rhetoric of "moral politics", which cloaks the maneuvers of states behind "the fight against the evil empire", "human rights", "freedom" or whatever, does not stand up to a reading of The *Prince*. And since democracy can only be nourished by the critical spirit of its citizens, we have to start by telling this truth, however bitter it may be.

But there's no despair in that. Losing your illusions doesn't prevent you from taking action - quite the contrary. For it is illusions that make effective action impossible. Belief in the magical power of empty words dispensed by moral teachers has never won a single battle. *The Prince* is not just a description of the means of politics. It also indicates the ends - those which alone justify these means - namely "civil life", the peace and security of citizens and the freedom of the fatherland. The men we still honor (de Gaulle, leader of the Resistance, for example) were "princes". Who can fail to see how much we need a prince, a collective prince in Gramsci's sense of the word, at a time when the accumulating threats threaten to undermine everything we hold dear?

Bibliography

MACHIAVELLI (Nicolas), *Œuvres*, translation by Christian Bec, Robert Laffont, "Bouquins", 1999.

GRAMSCI (Antonio), *Quaderni del carcere*, critical edition by Valentino Gerratana, 4 volumes, Einaudi, 2007.

HEGEL (Georg Wilhelm Friedrich), *The Constitution of Germany*, in *Écrits politiques*, translated from the German by Michel Jacob, Éditions Champ Libre, 1977.

LUCHAIRE (Jean), *Les Démocraties italiennes*, Flammarion, 1920.

ROUSSEAU (Jean-Jacques), *Œuvres III*, Gallimard, "La Pléiade", 1964.

SOREL (Georges), *Matériaux d'une théorie du prolétariat (1918)*, UQAC, "Classiques des sciences sociales", digital edition, 2003.

SOREL (Georges), *Réflexions sur la violence (1912)*, Marcel Rivière, 1936.

SPINOZA (Baruch), *Traité politique*, LGF/Le Livre de Poche, 2002.

Table of contents

Introduction: Machiavelli's Bad Reputation 7
The Prince, A Foundational Book of Modern Political Thought 11
The Hardest Part: Founding a New Principality ... 23
Republics have a Taste for Freedom 29
The Virtue a Prince Needs to Triumph 33
Caesar Borgia, A Prince with Two Faces 37
Cruelty is a necessary Evil 47
Choose the lesser of Two Evils 53
Only "Armed Prophets" Triumph 59
Don't confuse Moral Virtue with Political Virtue ... 65
Half Man, Half Beast 77
Keeping up Appearances: The Art of Governing is an Art of Communication 83

The People must be Satisfied 89

Necessary Evil 93

History Proves the Victors Right 99

The Ultimate Goal: To Liberate the Nation 103

Why does the republican Machiavelli take
on the Persona of the Prince? 109

Conclusion: Against Moralistic Preaching,
A Political Thought for Today 117

Bibliography 119

Best sellers Max Milo Editions

Hitler's banker, Jean-François Bouchard

Confessions of a forger, Éric Piedoie Le Tiec

The Koran and the flesh, Ludovic-Mohamed Zahed

Governing by fake news, Jacques Baud

Governing by chaos, Collectif

A political history of food, Paul Ariès

Mad in U.S.A.: The ravages of the "American model", Michel Desmurget

Mondial soccer club geopolitics, Kévin Veyssière

Putin: Game master?, Jacques Braud

Treatise on the three impostors: Moses, Jesus, Muhammad, The Spirit of Spinoza

TV Lobotomy, Michel Desmurget